# THE SECRET WORLD OF

# Spiders

# THE SECRET WORLD OF

# Spiders

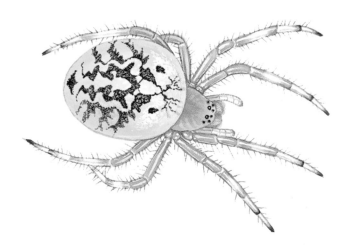

Theresa Greenaway

RAINTREE
STECK-VAUGHN
PUBLISHERS

A Harcourt Company

Austin   New York
www.raintreesteckvaughn.com

Published by Raintree Steck-Vaughn Publishers, an imprint of Steck-Vaughn Company

Acknowledgments
Project Editor: Kathryn Walker
Art Director: Max Brinkmann
Illustrated by Tim Hayward and Stuart Lafford
Designed by Ian Winton

Planned and produced by Discovery Books

Library of Congress Cataloging-in-Publication Data
Greenaway, Theresa, 1947-
Spiders / Theresa Greenaway.
p. cm. -- (The Secret World of--)
Includes bibliographical references (p. ).
ISBN 0-7398-3509-2
1. Spiders--Juvenile literature. [1. Spiders.] I. Title.
QL458.4 .G74 2001
595.4'4--dc21

00-062831

Printed and bound in the United States
1 2 3 4 5 6 7 8 9 LB 05 04 03 02 01

# Contents

# CHAPTER 1
# Life on Eight Legs

The biggest spider in the world is the South American tarantula, with a 3–inch (75 mm)–long body and legs spanning 10 inches (255 mm).

The smallest spiders are tinier than a pinhead. They live among damp moss or leaf litter.

Many spiders live for only 1 to 2 years, but tarantulas can live for as long as 20 years!

An irrational fear of spiders is called arachnophobia.

Spiders are still surprising scientists. In 1989, a completely new kind was found in a Romanian cave.

Many spiders do not have a common name. They only have the Latin name given to them by scientists. This is written in *italic letters* in this book.

Spiders belong to the group of animals called the arachnids. This group also includes scorpions, harvestmen (daddy long legs), mites, and ticks. The arachnids are part of a larger group of animals called the arthropods. All arthropods have jointed legs and a tough outer layer called the cuticle or exoskeleton. This does not stretch, so in order to grow, an arthropod has to shed its skin from time to time. This process is called molting.

**Spinnerets**
Tiny projections from which silk threads are drawn.

**Abdomen**
Rear part of body.

Insects, centipedes, and crabs, as well as arachnids, are arthropods. Arachnids are arthropods that have eight legs.

It is easy to tell the difference between spiders and insects – insects have only six legs, and usually have wings. Spiders never have wings!

A spider's body has two sections, connected by a narrow waist. The head and thorax, to which all the legs are attached, are joined together to make up the front section, called the cephalothorax. The eyes, jaws, and mouth, together with a pair of short feeler-like palps, are at the front of the head. The back part of the spider is called the abdomen. The abdomen contains the gut, reproductive and other organs, and the silk glands. At its tip are spinnerets from which silk is drawn wherever the spider goes. A spider has no bones. Its whole body is supported by a tough outer layer called a cuticle.

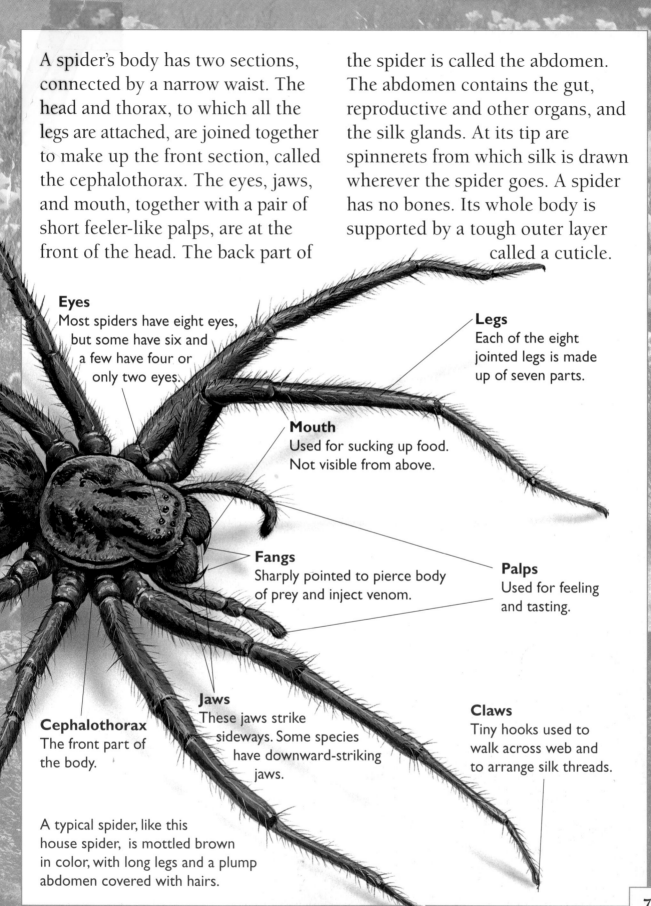

**Eyes**
Most spiders have eight eyes, but some have six and a few have four or only two eyes.

**Legs**
Each of the eight jointed legs is made up of seven parts.

**Mouth**
Used for sucking up food. Not visible from above.

**Fangs**
Sharply pointed to pierce body of prey and inject venom.

**Palps**
Used for feeling and tasting.

**Cephalothorax**
The front part of the body.

**Jaws**
These jaws strike sideways. Some species have downward-striking jaws.

**Claws**
Tiny hooks used to walk across web and to arrange silk threads.

A typical spider, like this house spider, is mottled brown in color, with long legs and a plump abdomen covered with hairs.

Almost all spiders have venom-injecting bites, so they can kill their prey. Many people are afraid of spiders, but there is really no need to fear most of them. The fangs of most spiders are too small and weak to penetrate our skin. Of those spiders with fangs that can, only a few kinds have venom that is potent enough to be dangerous to humans.

Spiders can thrive wherever there are insects for them to eat. Spiders live in almost all parts of the world, except in the sea, in frozen Antarctica, and on the highest mountain tops. A few live within the Arctic Circle, and some spiders live as far south as the islands of South Georgia, near Antarctica. There are spiders in

The female black widow spider has venom that is powerful enough to kill an adult human. She is easily recognized by the red "hourglass" marking on the underside of her abdomen.

deserts, tropical jungles, meadows, woodlands, and caves. There are even spiders that live in or on lakes and ponds, and, as we all know, many spiders live inside our houses.

## SPIDER JAWS

The jaws of this tarantula strike downward, so that the fangs stab into the victim.

The jaws of this wolf spider strike sideways like pincers.

## DIFFERENT KINDS OF SPIDERS

There are over 30,000 different species, or kinds, of spiders. These are divided into two main groups: spiders with jaws that strike downward and spiders with jaws that strike sideways, like pincers. Tarantulas (sometimes called bird-eating spiders), trapdoor spiders, and funnel-web spiders belong to the first group.

There are at least 2,000 different species of jumping spiders.

Some spiders are brightly colored to match the petals of a flower, so that insects cannot see them.

There are at least 2,600 kinds of orb weaver spiders.

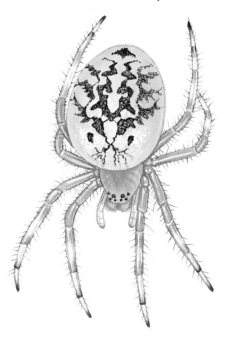

All other spiders have jaws that strike sideways. Over 90 families belong to this second group, including wolf spiders, jumping spiders, comb-footed spiders, recluse spiders, orb-web spiders, money spiders, crab spiders – and many others!

## EYES

Most spiders have eight tiny eyes, with one main pair and three secondary pairs. The rest have six, four, or two eyes. Although this seems like a lot of eyes, in fact a spider's eyesight is usually rather poor. Many kinds can tell only whether it is light or dark. Jumping and wolf spiders are exceptions. Their main eyes face forward and can focus on objects up to 7 inches (18 cm) away. The secondary eyes are on the sides of the head. These give the spiders a good field of view and enable them to judge distances.

Six of a wolf spider's eyes face forward, and two are on the top of the head. These can see out to the sides and a short distance behind the spider.

## GOOD VIBRATIONS

Spiders do not have ears, but they are very sensitive to vibrations. These are picked up, or detected, with special hairs on the spider's legs. These are connected to nerves that carry messages to its simple brain. A few, such as the male buzzing spider, produce vibrations that people can hear. These are made to attract females. As well as being able to pick up vibrations, the legs and palps of a spider help it taste its food and identify its surroundings.

# Sharing Your Home

Houses attract flies, mosquitoes, and other kinds of insects, so it is not surprising that spiders also move in. Long-legged cellar spiders make untidy webs up near the ceiling and under shelves.

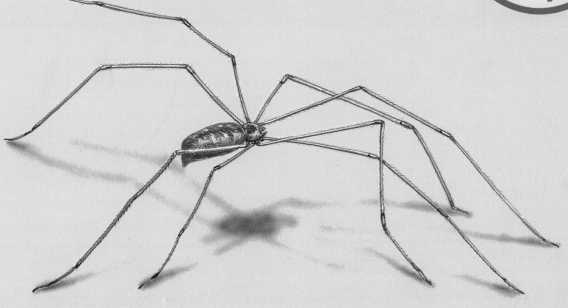

House spiders live lower down, behind cupboards, in basements, and in other dark nooks and crannies. This is the spider that causes alarm when it climbs into the bath overnight and cannot get out!

# CHAPTER 2
# Spider Silk

- The silk that a golden silk spider uses to make its dragline is the strongest natural fiber.

- The diameter of spider silk is about one-ten-thousandth of an inch (0.003 mm).

- A golden silk spider can make a continuous line of silk 2,300 feet (700 m) long.

- Comb-footed and orb weaver spiders make sticky silk for parts of their webs.

- Spider silk is as strong as nylon thread but is much more elastic.

- It would take 27,648 female garden spiders to make 1 pound (0.5 kg) of silk.

A spider's silk is very useful. It can be used to trap prey and to stop it from escaping, to line burrows, and to make a shelter under a leaf. A female spider uses her silk to wrap up her eggs; a male spider uses silk during mating. All spiders leave a line of silk, called a dragline, wherever they go. This means that if they jump from a twig to escape sudden danger, or they are knocked from their perch by a passing animal, they can get safely back home by climbing up the dragline.

Silk is produced in glands inside a spider's abdomen. It consists of a protein called fibroin. Inside the

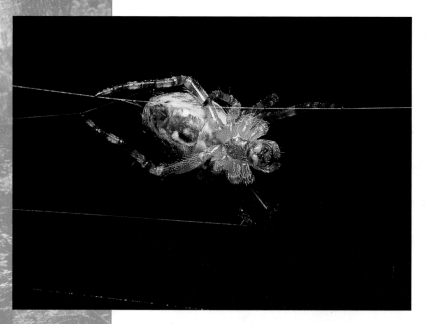

This female orb weaver spider is using her feet to hold the strands of silk and attach them in exactly the right place to start her web.

silk glands, fibroin is liquid.
It trickles
down the
finger-like spinnerets and is pulled
out by the spider's feet. As it is
pulled, the liquid silk solidifies
into strands. The spider uses its
feet to make it into sheets, webs,
or egg sacs.

## SPINNERETS

A spider has tiny, finger-like
projections called spinnerets at the
tip of its abdomen. Silk is drawn
out of the spinnerets through tiny
holes. Most kinds of spiders have
three pairs of spinnerets. The rest
have two pairs. The third pair has
become a pair of flat plates that

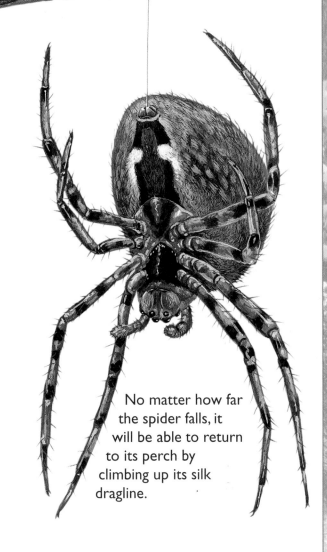

No matter how far
the spider falls, it
will be able to return
to its perch by
climbing up its silk
dragline.

contain as many as 40,000 even
smaller holes. The silk that is pulled
through these is the finest of all
spider silk. It is called "hackled"
silk. It is not sticky,
but because it is so fine, it
immediately clings to an insect's
legs and body.

A droplet of liquid silk trickles from each tiny
hole in the spider's spinnerets. It pulls each of
these into a fine silk thread.

13

## NIMBLE FOOTWORK

As a spider spins its silk into a web, or wraps up a fresh victim, it manipulates the silk threads with tiny hooks on each foot. With these, it can arrange each thread in exactly the right place, and it can also move about over its own silk threads without getting tangled.

Spiders that do not make webs have two tiny hooks on their feet, but web builders have three. The third claw presses the silk strands against barbed hairs, enabling the spider to construct its intricate webs. Tufts of hairs on some spiders' feet also help them to cling to upright or very smooth surfaces without falling.

The foot of this web-building spider has two hooklike toothed claws and a smaller third claw. This third claw holds the silk by pressing it against tufts of hairs.

## BALLOONING

If you look up into the air on a warm summer's afternoon, the

Very small spiders and spiderlings release long lines of silk that are pulled by breezes. The tiny spiders can then drift for long distances, spreading out to find new places to live.

chances are that you will see the sunlight glint on drifting lengths of spider silk. Or you may be startled when a sheet web spider lands on your arm, apparently out of nowhere. In fact, the sheet web spider has been drifting in the air on the end of a stretch of its silk. This habit is known as ballooning. Young spiderlings of many kinds "balloon" in order to move about, but adult sheet web spiders are still small enough to "balloon" from place to place.

I DIDN'T KNOW THAT

## Underwater Spider

The European water spider actually lives underwater, but it still needs to breathe and feed in air. It spins a silk sheet among water plants and carries air bubbles from the surface that it stores beneath the sheet to make an air-filled dome. Air is carried between the spider's back legs and abdomen. The spider lives in its air-filled tent, only leaving to catch prey or bring more air down from above.

# CHAPTER 3
# Wonderful Webs

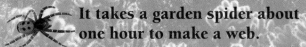

It takes a garden spider about one hour to make a web.

Tropical golden silk spiders make webs almost 6 feet (2 m) across with silk so strong it catches bats and small birds.

The biggest webs of all are built by social spiders that live together in large colonies. They combine webs to make one enormous web.

A colony of Panamanian social spiders may contain as many as 10,000 spiders!

A bolas spider puts a blob of sticky silk on the end of a line of silk and swings this to catch flying moths!

A spider's web is a clever trap for catching insects and other small animals. Different kinds of spiders construct very different kinds of webs. The simplest web of all is no more than silk trip-lines stretching out from the entrance of a silk tube. Other spiders make much more complex webs. Some look like sheets of silk, and others are three-dimensional tangles of threads. Most amazing of all are the beautifully constructed orb webs hung in just the right place to catch flying insects. When a spider has made its web, all it has to do is wait patiently for an unsuspecting victim to blunder into it. When this happens, the captive's struggles alert the spider to dart out and seize it.

Sticky silk has droplets of gluey liquid strung out all along it.

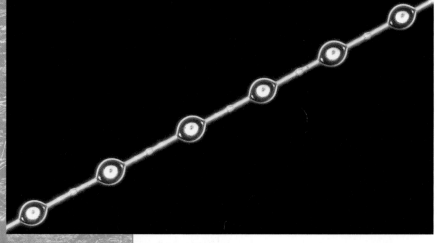

Feather-legged and garden spiders have extra tricks to make their webs even better at snaring their next meal. Feather-legged spiders make parts of their webs with extremely fine "hackled" silk. The hairs and hooks on an insect's feet get really tangled up in this. Garden spiders make the "spokes" of their orb webs of dry silk, but the spiral threads are made of sticky silk. Sticky silk comes from

Dewdrops clinging to the silk of this garden spider's web reveal the spokes and the spiral threads of this insect-catching net.

special silk glands. As the spider weaves it into a web, it twangs each thread, causing the sticky coating to separate into droplets. An insect's feet get stuck in this, but the spider does not. The spider walks only on the dry, non-sticky silk of the radiating spokes!

17

## SCAFFOLD WEBS

Comb-footed spiders build scaffold webs. These untidy webs are made of a central tangle of threads that is attached to nearby plant stems by other tightly stretched threads. The threads are strung with gluey droplets, rather like tiny beads.

Untidy scaffold webs are a mass of sticky threads stretching across twigs and leaves in order to trap the small flying insects that also live or feed among the foliage.

When an insect blunders into the tightly stretched threads, they break and contract, carrying the insect into the middle of the sticky web.

Sheet-web weavers dart out from their hiding place the instant they detect anything that twitches the silk threads of their "sheet."

## SHEETS AND HAMMOCKS

Sheet-web weavers make webs that look just like sheets of silk covering the ground or plants. At one end of the sheet, the spider makes a tunnel of silk, tucked under a rock or between plant stems, where it waits for something to land on its web.

Dwarf spiders also construct sheets of web, but these are found higher up among plant stems or grasses. The sheet is more like a hammock, with strands of silk stretching from the top of the sheet and into the surrounding vegetation. An insect colliding with these upper threads falls onto the hammock and is seized by the spider.

Sheet web spiders are common in grassy places, where they spin their small hammock-like webs between the grass stems. The spider bites its prey from below and drags it through the web.

## Throwing a Net

Ogre-eyed spiders spin a little web of stretchy silk that they hold out between their front three pairs of legs. The back legs hold onto a strand of silk so that the spider is hanging upside down, just a few inches above the ground. When an insect walks or flies below the spider, it drops the net over its victim.

## ORB WEBS

An orb web is an almost circular net. Spiders choose gaps between plant stems or corners of buildings to construct these webs. They have a framework of threads that radiate out like the spokes of a bicycle wheel. These are connected by spiral threads to make the net. The way in which an orb-web spider builds its web is fascinating. First, the spider pulls a thread of silk that is carried in the air until it makes contact with a nearby stem. The spider reinforces this with a bridge line. From the bridge line, the spider makes a Y-shape. The point where all three parts of the "Y" meet becomes the hub of the new web. More and more radial lines are made between the center and outer frame. The spider then spins the spiral. In the center of the web, where the spider often waits for a catch, the spiral is made of dry silk. The rest of the spiral is spun with thread coated with sticky droplets.

## PURSE WEBS

Instead of spinning a web that traps insects that blunder into it, the purse-web spider makes a silk tube, or purse, that lies on the surface of the ground. To disguise it, the spider covers the "purse" with fragments of dead leaves or twigs. The open end of the purse

## HOW AN ORB WEAVER SPIDER SPINS ITS WEB

1. The spider pulls a thread of silk and lets the breeze carry it to a twig. It then runs along this thread, reinforcing it with more silk.

2. The spider makes a Y-shaped framework below the first thread, and attaches to a lower twig.

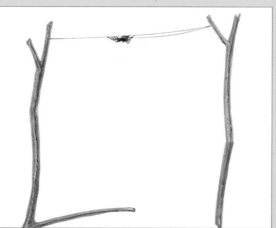

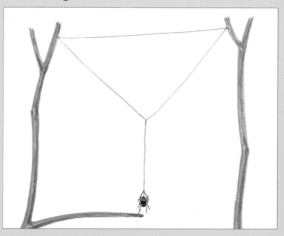

leads into a silk-lined, underground burrow. The spider waits inside until an insect walks over the purse. Then it stabs its prey through the silk wall of the purse and drags it into the burrow.

1. An unsuspecting insect walks over the dry leaves that hide the purse web.

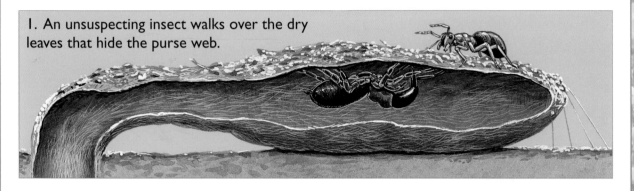

2. The purse-web spider bites its prey through the web, and pulls it inside.

3. Then the spider makes an outer frame, and starts to spin lines from the center of the web to the frame.

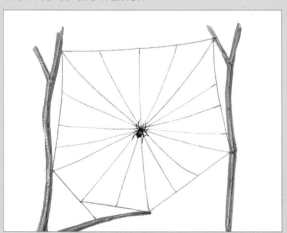

4. The spider spins a strengthening spiral, and finally, a spiral of sticky threads that will catch its prey.

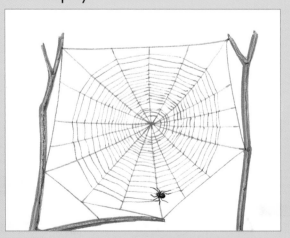

# CHAPTER 4
# Hunters

**A jumping spider can leap up to 40 times its own length.**

**A wolf spider catches and eats between 5 and 15 small insects a day.**

**A little jumping spider eats about six insects a day, including plant-eating leaf-hoppers.**

All spiders are predators that need to catch live prey, but only some of them are active hunters. If you watch a woodpile or rocky outcrop on a sunny day, the dull brown or blackish spiders that you see running over it in short, fast sprints are mostly wolf spiders. They have good eyesight and are on the look-out for movements that may indicate a suitable meal is close by. A catch is made after a combination of creeping and sprinting, with a final pounce onto the victim. As you are watching wolf spiders, you might find that a jumping spider or a lynx spider is watching you!

Spiders that hunt at night have poor eyesight and rely on other senses to find and catch their prey. They live under wood, leaf litter, or in crevices in buildings. They find slow-moving insects and other invertebrates by feeling around with their front legs.

Wolf spiders, like this one from Arizona, can run quickly over the ground both to catch prey and to escape from danger.

## JUMPING SPIDERS

Unlike the mostly dull–colored wolf spiders, jumping spiders are often brightly patterned. Although they are rather small spiders, their two main eyes are large and easy to see. Attracted by a moving insect, and able to see clearly how far away it is, these spiders catch their prey by leaping on it from quite considerable distances. Some can even make vertical leaps of up to 6 inches (15 cm). Their silk dragline stops them from falling to the ground. They simply run back up the line with their catch.

A jumping spider pushes off with its back legs and sails through the air. As it jumps, a dragline of silk is pulled from its spinnerets.

## STICKY SPIT

Spitting spiders have an unusual way of catching their prey. They are small spiders that have rather poor eyesight. When a fly lands nearby, or the spider manages to creep up close, it traps its prey by spitting a jet of sticky liquid from each jaw. By rapidly moving its head from side to side as it is spitting, the spider pins down the insect with two zigzags of gum. Then the spitting spider can kill and eat its prey.

The woodlouse spider prefers to stay hidden, but be warned. If you pick one up, its powerful fangs give a painful bite.

## SLOW BUT TOUGH

Slow-moving woodlice rely on a hard outer layer like armor plating to keep them safe. The woodlouse spider specializes in catching and eating these crustaceans. It catches woodlice by piercing their armor plating with particularly hard, sharp fangs. It twists sideways to bite the woodlouse so that one fang pierces the softer underside, and the other fang stabs through the upper side.

## LYING IN WAIT

Female crab spiders have plump bodies that are white, greenish, yellow, or even pink. They sit in flowers waiting to ambush visiting insects. Often they choose a flower that matches their color, but sometimes they get it wrong and sit on petals of quite the wrong shade! They are able to change color slightly over a few days to get a better match.

Perfectly matched with the yellow buttercup, this crab spider is ready to catch any other insect that visits this flower.

# Tiny Thieves

Tiny *Argyrodes* spiders live on the webs of other kinds of spiders. They feed on insects that are caught in their host's web. The true owner of the web is often a much larger spider and may not bother to eat the small insects that get caught in its web, so the intruder keeps the web tidy. But these tiny spiders also feed on the host's prey and, on occasion, kill and eat their host!

I DIDN'T KNOW THAT

# CHAPTER 5
# After the Catch

When an insect is caught in a web, it struggles violently to escape. If it is really lucky, it manages to tear a large hole in the web and breaks free. Most captives are not so fortunate. Within about five seconds, the spider has run from its lair and bitten its victim. Many insects could sting or bite the spider. To prevent this, a spider has to overcome its victim quickly. Each bite injects droplets of venom that swiftly paralyze or kill the insect.

**Black widow spider** – Females of this timid spider have venom about 15 times more powerful than rattlesnake venom, but the amount injected is far smaller. It can cause death in humans, but there is now an antidote to counteract its harmful effects.

**Sydney funnel-web spider** – This Australian spider will attack anything close to it that moves, and its fangs can even go through fingernails. Bites have caused death in as little as 15 minutes.

**Brazilian wandering spider** – This aggressive spider, with a 5–inch (13–cm) legspan and the biggest venom glands of all spiders, will run at people to inflict its dangerous bite.

**Recluse spider** – Bites from recluse spiders are slow to heal and can cause death. They are not aggressive spiders but are often found in houses.

The spider takes no chances. While its venom is taking effect, the butterfly is wrapped in a wide band of silk so that it cannot struggle free.

The venom is produced in glands at the base of each jaw. When the spider bites, muscles contract and squeeze the glands, so that venom trickles down canals inside each fang and out through small holes at the tip. The sharply pointed fangs penetrate weak spots in an insect's tough outer coat, and the venom acts quickly. A spider may wait until it has taken effect, but orb-web spiders and some others immediately start to wrap their catch in bands of silk.

Bites from some spiders can be fatal to people, especially small children. A few, such as the Brazilian wandering spider and the Sydney funnel-web spider, are aggressive and will really try to bite anyone that comes near. Others, even some of the most dangerous kinds, are really rather timid. Black widow and recluse spiders only bite people if they feel threatened. Unfortunately, accidents occur when these spiders enter houses and hide in beds or among clothing. They may not be seen by someone climbing into bed or pulling on a sweatshirt.

This highly venomous Sydney funnel-web spider is in a characteristic threat position. It has raised its front legs and its palps, and a drop of venom glistens on the tip of each fang.

When they are pressed between cloth and skin, black widow spiders and recluse spiders bite to protect themselves.

It is important for anyone who has been bitten by a dangerously venomous spider to get medical attention quickly. However, it is also important to remember that most kinds of spiders are harmless. Only about 500 of the thousands and thousands of different species have fangs that are strong enough to penetrate human skin, and of these, less than 30 have venom potent enough to affect a human.

## LIQUIDIZERS

Spiders eat only liquid or semi-liquid food. A spider's fangs cannot slice up and chew prey, although on the base of each jaw there are sometimes small teeth that can crush prey. When venom is injected, digestive juices also enter the body of the victim. These juices get to work on the soft internal organs, turning them into a mushy soup. The spider sucks up this soup, leaving all the hard parts of the prey. After a crab spider has fed, just an empty husk is left, but

Wandering spiders search for food by night, and they are large enough to catch and eat big insects such as katydids and even small tree frogs. This species is not dangerous to humans.

spiders that crush their prey while the digestive juices are taking effect leave a shapeless mass.

Food is drawn down the spider's throat by the action of the sucking stomach. Any solid fragments get caught on hairs that grow in the mouth and throat. These are eventually spat out.

### VARIED DIET

Most spiders eat insects, and some feed on other small invertebrates. Those that spin webs catch flying insects and crawling kinds that accidentally fall into their webs. But the spider will not eat everything that becomes tangled in its web. A small spider may cut the silk around a stinging bee or wasp so that it falls from the web. Some insects produce foul smells or spray out unpleasant liquids to deter predators such as spiders. These are also rejected.

Trapdoor spiders lie in wait for prey inside their burrow. They dart out and snatch anything that walks over their trapdoor. Once they have taken their prey inside, they decide whether it is good to eat or not. Grasshoppers, beetles, or shieldbugs that produce foul smells are quickly thrown out of the burrow unharmed.

## Snake eaters

Large tarantulas may occasionally eat birds, but they mostly eat frogs, lizards, and small snakes. In captivity, a *Grammostola* spider killed and ate a venomous rattlesnake 18 inches (46 cm) long! Mice and young rats are also eaten if the spider can catch them.

I DIDN'T KNOW THAT

# CHAPTER 6
# Reproduction

A large female tarantula lays up to 3,000 eggs in one clutch.

The tiny *Oonops* spider lays just two eggs at a time.

A female golden silk spider may weigh 100 times more than her mate.

The male crab spider spins silk around the female so she is tied down while they mate.

Male grass spiders hold the jaws of their mate open so that the females cannot bite them.

Male and female spiders must get together to mate. Only then can a female lay the fertile eggs that will hatch into the next generation of spiders. A male spider has to approach a female cautiously. He is usually much smaller than she is and does not want to be mistaken for prey. A female spider is bigger than her mate because her body has to contain the eggs until they are ready to be laid. Some female spiders do indeed eat their mates, but, since males usually die shortly after mating, this means that their bodies are not wasted.

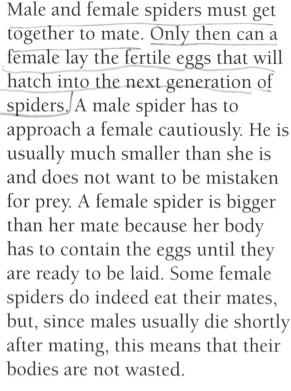

A male golden orb spider is so much smaller than the female that he is not worth eating. He is at no risk as he crosses her web and mates with her.

The nutrients they contain help to produce a large clutch of developing eggs. Even if they do not fall prey to their hungry mates, male spiders play no part in caring for their young.

Male spiders use several ways to advertise their arrival. If their approach is accepted, they come closer and stroke the female with their front legs. This subdues her, so that mating can take place. After mating, a lucky male leaves and may start courting another. Inside the female, the eggs start to develop.

The male garden spider is in danger of being eaten by his fat-bodied mate. He signals to her by vibrating his legs and tweaking her web.

## SIGNALS

Male jumping spiders and wolf spiders signal to their farsighted females by waving their front legs or palps. Sometimes these signals are accompanied by side to side movements or leg vibrations. *Zygiella* spiders vibrate the female's web to signal to each other. First the male plucks a strand of the female's web. Then she answers, also by plucking strands of her web.

## EGG LAYING

Before laying her eggs, a female spider spins a small sheet of silk. This may be flat or cup-shaped. When it is ready, she lays her clutch of eggs on the silk sheet. The eggs and the sheet on which they were laid are now enclosed in more silk to make an egg sac. A long-legged cellar spider makes a flimsy egg sac that she holds in her jaws until the spiderlings hatch.

This spider makes her egg sac in a curled leaf and then stands over it, but by the time the eggs hatch, she will have died.

Wolf spiders and many other kinds make a much tougher egg sac. Wolf spider mothers carry theirs around by holding them with their spinnerets. Sheet-web and lynx spiders are among those that stand guard over their egg sac until the eggs hatch.

## HATCHING

Inside each egg, a spider starts to develop, nourished by egg yolk. When it is ready to hatch, it tears the eggshell with a tiny egg tooth on its head. When first hatched, a

If anything disturbs these tiny garden spiders, they immediately scatter in all directions. This means that a predator will only be able to catch a few of them.

The tiny young spiders usually stay crowded together until after their second molt.

### CARING MOTHERS

After a female spider has laid her eggs, some take no further care of the egg sac at all, but many protect their precious eggs. Lynx, crab spiders, and others stand guard over their egg sacs. Wolf and swamp spiders are among those that carry their egg sacs around with them all the time.

The nursery-tent spider carries her egg sac gripped in her jaws. She chooses to sit in sunny places to keep it warm and dry.

tiny spiderling is unable to spin silk or catch prey. Until its first molt, it continues to feed on the rest of the yolk, safe inside the egg sac. Within a day or two, it molts and together with all the other spiderlings, leaves the egg sac.

*Pardosa* wolf spider mothers continue to care for their young even after they have hatched. The tiny spiderlings climb onto their mother's abdomen. She carries around her cluster of tiny babies until their second molt. Then the young spiderlings are ready to take care of themselves.

As her name suggests, a female nursery-tent spider spins a tent of silk over herself just before the

The abdomen of this female wolf spider is completely hidden by her brood of tiny young spiders. If one falls off, it just climbs back up its silk dragline.

spiderlings hatch. These tents are made between blades of grass, and the spiderlings cluster together inside the tent.

## HOW SPIDERS GROW

Young spiders are miniature versions of their parents, but they cannot mate and reproduce until they are adults. Their tough outer layer, the cuticle, is not very stretchy, so spiders have to molt in order to grow. The old skin splits along the sides. The spider wriggles to make the split larger and pulls out its eight legs. The damp, new cuticle is soft and stays

## Food Sharing

The female comb-footed spider produces a fluid in her mouth that her spiderlings feed on for several days. Then she shares her food with her tiny young. She crushes her prey so that they can feed on the liquids that ooze out.

stretchy until it dries. A freshly molted spider is larger than it was before. Skins that have been shed can often be seen hanging in spiders' webs. Once they are grown, most spiders no longer molt, but tarantulas, which live a long time, continue to molt even after they have become adults.

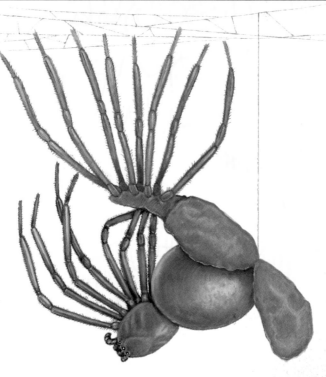

Molting is a dangerous time for a spider. Even after it has wriggled out of its old skin, it cannot run from danger until its new skin has hardened.

35

# CHAPTER 7
# Survival Tactics

The world is a hazardous place for spiders, because there are so many larger predators eager to eat them. Some kinds simply hide to keep out of harm. Huntsman spiders hide under bark or stones. Some make burrows or spin silk tubes or funnels. Trapdoor spiders close their burrows with lids, and a female trapdoor spider spends all her long life inside her burrow. Life is riskier for a male trapdoor spider, who has to leave his burrow to find a mate.

**The California trapdoor spider can hold the lid to its burrow shut even if a force 38 times its own weight is trying to pull it up.**

**The tropical crab spider looks exactly like a shiny fresh bird dropping that has just landed on a leaf.**

Blending in with a background of bark, leaves, or petals is another way of escaping the notice of a predator. This kind of disguise is called camouflage. Australian lichen spiders live and hunt on tree trunks covered with flaky patches of lichen. They are camouflaged to look just like the lichen-covered bark. Some crab spiders are the same color as flower petals. Tropical lynx spiders sit in the middle of leaves, but they are hard to spot because they are bright green, just like the leaf.

This goldenrod spider can change color to match the flower on which it sits. It can even turn pink. As long as it keeps still, a sharp-eyed predator will not see it.

Lynx spiders often have bright green bodies with brown markings, just like the leaves on which they hide.

birds into thinking that they are something more dangerous, like a stinging wasp.

### CONCEALED ENTRANCE

Trapdoor spiders close their burrows with a variety of ingenious hinged lids. These help to hide the burrows, and so protect the spider. The burrows are sometimes over 12 inches (30 cm) deep, and are dug by the spider using its jaws. The spider makes the wall smooth with a mixture of mud and saliva and lines it with silk. The tightly fitting lids are made of bits of bark, soil, or twigs, bound together with silk.

Another kind of disguise is known as mimicry. By looking like another kind of animal altogether, spiders trick predators such as

Pointed projections on the back of this bark spider are a good imitation of the spines on the twig. The spider is also the same color as the twig, which makes it very difficult to detect.

Some Australian trapdoor spiders have secret side chambers or emergency exits from their burrows. The pellet spider is even more ingenious. As well as a trapdoor at the entrance, this spider digs a shallow side chamber halfway down the burrow. It makes a pear-shaped "pellet" from mud, saliva, and silk and places this in the side chamber. If anything enters its burrow, it pulls on the silk to flip the pellet so that it blocks the lower part of the burrow, in which the spider is hiding.

When a trapdoor spider wants to leave its burrow, it lifts the closely fitting lid and cautiously looks out. If it detects danger, it darts back inside, pulling the lid shut.

## ARMOR PLATING

A burrow can become a dangerous place if a spider suddenly finds itself trapped inside. To keep predators from pulling a *Cyclocosmia truncata* spider from its burrow, it has a thick, very tough shield on the end of its abdomen. This can be used to plug the narrow end at the bottom of the burrow.

## MASTERS OF MIMICRY

Many birds eat spiders, but fewer eat stinging ants because if there is one ant there are usually hundreds, swarming all over the place. Jumping spiders gain protection from these birds by looking just like ants. They even

# Itchy Hairs

Tarantulas have very hairy legs and bodies. The hairs are barbed and break off easily, so if a spider is attacked by an enemy, it scratches off clouds of these hairs from its back and flicks them into the enemy's face. They stick in and make the thin skin of the nose and mouth of predators very itchy. They also irritate human skin.

wave their front pair of legs as an ant waves its antennae (feelers), and they run about like ants as well.

A jumping spider from Borneo mimics a wasp in an unusual way. The front part of the spider looks like the wasp's abdomen, and the rear of the spider's abdomen looks like the wasp's head. The spider's spinnerets mimic wasp feelers and jaws. If a predator attacks the "false"

head, the spider can cause confusion by running away in reverse.

The abdomen of this jumping spider is shaped to look like a wasp's head and thorax. The spider's real head is at the top left of the picture.

# CHAPTER 8
# Spiders Under Threat

Even though a female spider may lay hundreds of eggs, few survive long enough to reproduce. Spiders encounter many dangers, even the largest kinds. Some simply die of starvation or lack of water. Many are eaten by birds. Others are eaten by small mammals, lizards, frogs, toads, or even pet cats. Yet others have a more sinister fate. They are eaten by wasp grubs while they are still alive.

People also pose threats to spiders. Rain forest spiders are under threat because every year more and more

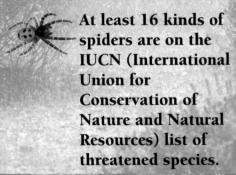

The Mexican red-kneed spider, a kind of tarantula, has become so popular as a pet it is protected under CITES (Convention on International Trade in Endangered Species).

At least 16 kinds of spiders are on the IUCN (International Union for Conservation of Nature and Natural Resources) list of threatened species.

The no-eyed big-eyed wolf spider, known also as the Kauai cave wolf spider, is possibly the most threatened spider in the United States.

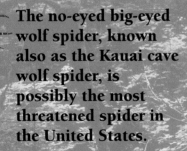

Male trapdoor spiders are in greatest danger when they leave the safety of their burrows to search for a female.

Pesticide used to spray these orange trees to kill harmful insects also kills the spiders that would eat these insects.

This spider looks dead, but it is not. It has just been paralyzed by the wasp's sting. The spider will be eaten alive by the wasp's grub.

of the forest is felled by people. Some kinds of large tarantulas have become rare because too many have been collected so that people can keep them as pets.

The use of insecticides on farms and in gardens is another hazard. Not only are spiders as well as insect pests killed by these chemicals, but they reduce the number of insects on which any surviving spiders can prey.

## WILY WASPS

Spider-hunting wasps fly low over the floors of tropical rain forests looking for tarantulas or the burrows in which they hide. When they find one, they paralyze it with a venomous sting. If it is not already in a burrow, the wasp drags it to its own burrow. The wasp lays a single egg on the spider's body. When the grub hatches, it feeds on the spider, slowly eating it alive.

## SPIDER-EATING BIRDS

Around the world, all sorts of small birds search treetops, bushes, under fallen leaves, in crevices of bark, around windows, and on lawns in their hunt for spiders, insects, and other invertebrates. Some specialize in eating spiders. The long-billed spiderhunter is one of 10 kinds of spiderhunters from southeast Asia that snatch spiders from their webs with their curved beaks, before they can run and hide.

## DEADLY DAMSELFLIES

The helicopter damselfly from Central America eats only spiders. These damselflies are very long but extremely thin, and their gauzy wings span 7½ inches (19 cm). They have good eyesight. When one spots a spider, it flutters a short distance away without being noticed. Then with a sudden burst of speed, it snatches the spider from its web, bites off the juicy abdomen, and lets the legs, head, and jaws fall.

## SPRING-CLEANING

The spiders that share our houses with us are in great danger from dusters, vacuum cleaners, and other household appliances. Almost all of these spiders do no harm at all to people, and even help to keep down insect invaders. But their webs can attract dust and make an annoying mess. So out they go!

Stonechats are just one of many kinds of small birds that search trees and bushes for spiders and insects to eat. However well-hidden, if the spider moves, then the bird will spot it.

# Treacherous Spiders

Many kinds of spiders will eat each other if they get the chance. Pirate spiders specialize in eating comb-footed spiders. These small spiders enter the comb-footed spider's web and pretend to be a struggling insect. When the spider rushes out, it is seized and killed by a very potent bite to one of its front legs. Young spiders may also eat each other if they cannot find other prey, and some kinds feed on the body of their dead mother. Most sinister of all is the habit of many female spiders, like this crab spider, of eating the unfortunate male either before or just after mating.

I DIDN'T KNOW THAT

# Glossary

**ABDOMEN** – The back part of a spider's body, containing the gut, reproductive and other organs, and the silk glands

**ANTIDOTE** – A substance that counteracts the effects of venom or poison

**ARACHNIDS** – A group of arthropods, all of which have four pairs of legs

**ARTHROPODS** – Invertebrate animals that have a tough outer layer called a cuticle, or exoskeleton, and jointed legs

**BALLOONING** – The way in which many small or young spiders float through the air on long threads of silk

**CAMOUFLAGE** – Colors or patterns that allow an animal to blend in with its background

**CEPHALOTHORAX** – The front section of a spider's body, made up of its head and thorax

**CUTICLE** – The tough outer layer, or exoskeleton, of a spider or insect that supports and protects the body within it

**DRAGLINE** – The line of silk spiders leave behind them wherever they go. It allows them to drop to the ground safely and to climb back up

**EGG SACS** – The silken case, or cocoon, in which the mother spider wraps her eggs

**FANGS** – Long, slender, pointed teeth through which venom is injected

**FIBROIN** – The protein from which spider silk is made

**HACKLED SILK** – The finest of all spider silk

**INVERTEBRATES** – Animals that do not have a backbone

**MIMICRY** – A protective feature in which one animal looks like another kind of animal or object, allowing it to trick predators into thinking that it is dangerous or undesirable to eat

**MOLT** – To shed the entire outer layer of skin

**PALPS** – The pair of short, feeler-like projections on each side of a spider's mouth

**PREDATOR** – An animal that catches and eats other animals

**PREY** – An animal that is caught and eaten by another animal

**SILK GLANDS** – The organs inside the spider's abdomen that produce silk

**SPIDERLING** – A young spider

**SPINNERETS** – The tiny finger-like projections at the tip of the spider's abdomen through which silk is drawn

**THORAX** – The part of the front section of a spider's body that bears its legs

**VENOM** – A toxic liquid injected into the body of another animal by means of fangs, claws, or stingers

**WEB** – The silken trap a spider weaves to catch its prey

# Further Reading

Burnie, David. *Insects and Spiders*. Alexandria, VA: Time-Life, 1997.

Clarke, Penny. *Insects and Spiders*. Danbury, CT: Franklin Watts, 1995.

Murray, Peter. *Spiders*. Chanhassen, MN: Childs World, 1991.

Squire, Ann. *Spiders of North America*. Danbury, CT: Franklin Watts, 2000.

Theodorou, Rod, and Telford, Carole. *Spider and Scorpion*. Chicago: Heinemann, 1998.

Acknowledgments
Front cover: Ken Preston-Mafham/Premaphotos Wildlife; p.8: Bruce Coleman Collection;
p.10 Anthony Bannister/Natural History Photographic Library; p.11 Dr Rod Preston-Mafham/Premaphotos Wildlife;
p.12: Harold Taylor ABIPP/Oxford Scientific Films; p.13 Dr Frieder Sauer/Bruce Coleman Collection; p.14: Harold Taylor
ABIPP/Oxford Scientific Films; p.15: Agence Nature/Natural History Photographic Agency; p.16: Alastair
Macewen/Oxford Scientific Films; p.17: Jane Burton/Bruce Coleman Collection; p.18: Stephen Dalton/Natural History
Photographic Agency; p.19: Ken Preston-Mafham/Premaphotos Wildlife; p.22: Alan Stillwell/Bruce Coleman Collection;
p.23: Bruce Coleman Collection; p.24 top: Ken Preston-Mafham/Premaphotos Wildlife; p.24 bottom: Ken Preston-
Mafham/Premaphotos Wildlife; p.25: Ken Preston-Mafham/Premaphotos Wildlife; p.26: Anthony Bannister/Natural
History Photographic Agency; p.27: Fritz Prenzel/Bruce Coleman Collection; p.28: M.P.L.Fogden/Bruce Coleman
Collection; p.29: Daniel Heuclin/Natural History Photographic Agency; p.30: A.N.T./Natural History Photographic
Agency; p.31: Jane Burton/Bruce Coleman Collection; p.32: Kim Taylor/Bruce Coleman Collection; p.33 top: Felix
Labhardt/Bruce Coleman Collection; p.33 bottom: Ken Preston-Mafham/Premaphotos Wildlife; p.34: Felix
Labhardt/Bruce Coleman Collection; p.35: Daniel Heuclin/Natural History Photographic Agency; p.37 top: John
Cancalosi/Bruce Coleman Collection; p.37 bottom: Waina Cheng Ward/Bruce Coleman Collection; p.38: Sean
Morris/Oxford Scientific Films; p.39: Daniel Heuclin/Natural History Photographic Agency; p.40: Chris Sharp/Oxford
Scientific Films; p.41: Ken Preston-Mafham/Premaphotos Wildlife; p.42: Jean-Louis le Moigne/Natural History
Photographic Agency; p.43: Andrew Purcell/Bruce Coleman Collection.

# Index

Numbers in *italic* indicate pictures